BMX

First American edition published in 2004
by LernerSports

This book is available in two editions:
Library binding by LernerSports
Soft cover by First Avenue Editions
Imprints of Lerner Publishing Group
241 First Avenue North
Minneapolis, MN 55401 U.S.A.

Website address: www.lernerbooks.com

Designed and produced by:
David West Children's Books
7 Princeton Court
55 Felsham Road
London, England

Designer: Gary Jeffrey
Editor: James Pickering
Picture Research: Carlotta Cooper

Library of Congress Cataloging-in-Publication Data

Job, Chris.
BMX / by Chris Job.
p. cm.—(Extreme Sports)
Includes index.
Summary: An introduction to BMX cycling's history, equipment, techniques, terms, styles, and stars.
ISBN: 0–8225–1243–2 (lib. bdg.)
ISBN: 0–8225–1193–2 (pbk.)
1. Bicycle motocross—Juvenile literature. [1. Bicycle motocross. 2. Bicycle racing. 3. Extreme Sports.] I. Title. II. Series.
GV1049.3 .J63 2004
796.6'2—dc21 2002151699

Bound in the United States of America
1 2 3 4 5 6 – OS – 09 08 07 06 05 04

PHOTO CREDITS :
Abbreviations: t-top, m-middle, b-bottom, r-right, l-left, c-center.

Front cover - Corbis. 3, 5, 10bl & br, 11 both, 12-13, 13tm & m, 17, 18l, 18-19t, 24-25b, 25 both, 29tl & r - Steve Jackson. 6 both, 7 both, 8 both, 9 both, 14t, 15t, 22, 23t, 24-25t, 26, 26-27, 28t, 29bl - James Hudson. 14br, 16, 20r, 21l, 23bm, 28b - Buzz Pictures. 19b - Damien Elliott / Dig Magazine. 20l - Corbis Images.

An explanation of difficult words can be found in the glossary on page 31.

extreme sports

BMX

Chris Job

LERNER SPORTS
AN IMPRINT OF LERNER PUBLISHING GROUP

CONTENTS

FLY LIKE A BIRD! Kicking his legs out behind him, this rider demonstrates the superman jump.

Introduction

BMX has its roots in late 1960s California. Early riders wanted to imitate motocross (motorcycle races on rough tracks). The term "Bicycle Motocross," or BMX for short, was coined. Many BMX styles soon developed. A rider might become a ramp rider, a dirt jumper, a flatlander, a street rider, or a racer. Although these styles of BMX differ, they all share the same roots.

13 FEET OF AIR

A vertical height pole proves that riders can leap, or "air," a full 13 feet (4 meters) above a ramp.

Sprite
SONY

WARNING!

BMX CAN BE AN **EXTREMELY DANGEROUS** SPORT. DO NOT TRY ANY MOVES **BEYOND YOUR ABILITIES** AND ALWAYS WEAR SAFETY EQUIPMENT.

Racing in the early 1970s was tricky. Twelve or more riders often competed at the same time. Heavy frames and plastic mudguards made the bikes difficult to control. Few people realized that less weight meant more speed.

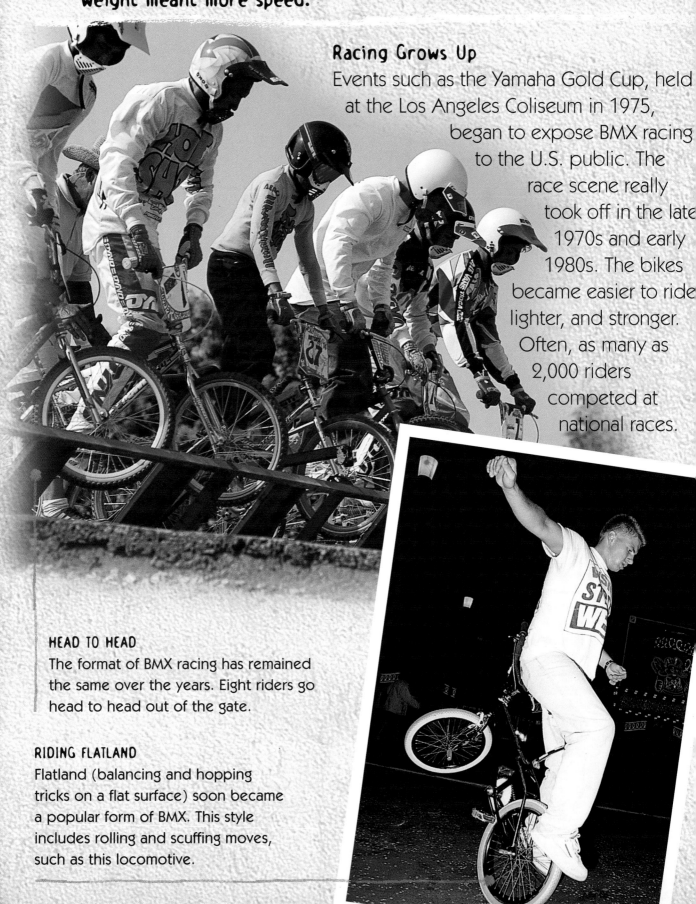

Racing Grows Up

Events such as the Yamaha Gold Cup, held at the Los Angeles Coliseum in 1975, began to expose BMX racing to the U.S. public. The race scene really took off in the late 1970s and early 1980s. The bikes became easier to ride, lighter, and stronger. Often, as many as 2,000 riders competed at national races.

HEAD TO HEAD
The format of BMX racing has remained the same over the years. Eight riders go head to head out of the gate.

RIDING FLATLAND
Flatland (balancing and hopping tricks on a flat surface) soon became a popular form of BMX. This style includes rolling and scuffing moves, such as this locomotive.

The Birth of Freestyle

Doing tricks and jumps (called freestyle riding) became more popular than racing. Whether showing off between races or fooling around in the park, riders could freestyle anywhere. Freestyle contests began to spring up in the early 1980s.

FOOTPLANT
Early freestylers wore racing gear but had their own style. Steve Grace demonstrates a footplant on a miniramp.

HALF-PIPES
Two curved walls make up a half-pipe. The walls slope gradually from flat to vertical. The slope, or arc, is called the transition.

Ramp and Street Riding

In the mid-1980s, riders grew frustrated with the rules of organized freestyle contests. As a result, riders found obstacles on the streets to ride. Skateboarding gave them ideas about where and what to ride, especially their half-pipe ramps.

To be a young BMX rider in the 1980s was great. Then a slump came at the end of the decade. Many decided that riding a 20-inch bike was not a grown-up thing to do.

Going Underground

In the early 1990s, riders began to specialize in one area of riding. Mat Hoffman and Dennis McCoy pushed ramp riding to the next level. Kevin Jones and Chase Gouin created moves that still look good.

FASTPLANT
Riders developed street moves like this fastplant—pushing the bike into the air with your foot.

HALF-PIPE PROGRESSION
Due to their dangerous moves, some riders went through a bike a week. Here, Carlo Griggs kicks his feet into a position called a no-footed candy bar.

GUIDE #1

RIDER-OWNED COMPANIES
Companies like Standard, S&M, Homeless Bikes, Hoffman, and 2-Hip were among the first rider-owned companies. Mat Hoffman and Ron Wilkerson were company founders, as well as contest organizers. Their work with riders such as Joe Johnson and Brian Blyther helped to shape the sport of BMX.

FOUNDING FATHERS
From left, Johnson, Hoffman, Wilkerson, and Blyther.

THE CHASM!
Between 1992 and 1997, the Backyard Jams signified the rebirth of BMX. Here, Fuzzy Hall clears the traditional big jump—the chasm.

Emerging from the Gloom

At the start of the 1990s, BMX competitions were low-key affairs. But in 1995, thousands of people watched riders compete in the X Games. BMX began to return to the public eye. A whole new breed of riders got into the sport. The Backyard Jam attracted about 4,000 spectators with minimal advertising.

Safety Equipment

You will discover when you take up BMX that you spend lots of time rolling around on the ground. No matter what area of BMX you choose, falling off and injuries are part of the package.

Fearless Riders

The crash section of a BMX video reveals that few tricks are pulled off the first time. The risk of injuries can be minimized by riding realistically. It takes many hours in the saddle to learn to fall properly. Protecting yourself can mean sliding onto knee pads, pushing the bike away, or running out of a jump. None of these things comes naturally!

PAYING THE PRICE
Even when fully protected, injuries happen. Here, Dave Mirra dons an ice pack between runs.

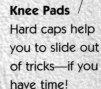

Knee Pads
Hard caps help you to slide out of tricks—if you have time!

Knee/Shin Combos
These can save you a great deal of pain.

What to Wear?

Choosing the right safety gear for a ride is fairly obvious. It's easy to remain well protected but still look normal. The golden rule is to ride sensibly and appreciate the risks.

Helmet
A heavy blow weakens a helmet, and it should be replaced.

Gloves
Minor hand scrapes can stop you from riding but are easily preventable.

Read about the history of BMX, watch some videos, and try out a friend's bike. Then what? You need to get a bike and learn to ride it right.

Get the Right Bike

It's a big mistake to buy the wrong bike. Avoid buying a so-called BMX from a catalog. It's probably a cheap imitation of a BMX. A BMX shop will be able to recommend plenty of well-designed bikes made by well-known companies. They can also advise you on which bikes fit your style of riding.

UNFAMILIAR
The low seat and small wheels will make your BMX feel strange at first.

The Bunny Hop

The bunny hop is the basic trick of BMX riding. It unlocks virtually every trick in the sport. If you learn the bunny hop, you'll be able to jump higher and get out of the top of ramps. It's also the first part of countless street moves.

BUNNY HOP KEY

1. Approach the object at a reasonable pace.
2. As you near the object, pull up the front wheel.
3. Begin to shift your weight forward.
4. Pull up the back end by tucking in your legs.
5. Pushing forward on the bars helps straighten the bike in the air.
6. Lower the back end with your legs to bring it in for the landing.

1.
2.
3.

GUIDE #2

BIKE DESIGN

Brake Cable
Detangler
Detangler This simple but clever device allows the handlebars to be turned 360 degrees without the brake cables becoming tangled.
Frame Gussets These metal plates are welded to the frame for strength without adding much weight.
Decent Tires High-pressure tires protect your wheels from dents. A strong sidewall stops the inner tube from poking through.
Dropouts and Socket Pegs Dropouts are where the wheels connect to the frame. With pegs (strong metal tubes), these protect the bike.

4.
5.
6.

Trying a Style

As bike riding evolved, a few broad styles emerged. There's ramp, street, flat, and dirt. Once you learn the basics about your bike and riding, you should try out the different styles to see which one suits you.

STREET RIDING
Use the world around you to ride the way you want—even up a tree.

Dedication

Many riders dedicate themselves to one form of riding. They make their mark on that style with the way they ride, with their bike setup, and with their general attitude toward the sport. Only some riders are willing to try more than one style of riding. Experiment before you eliminate any style from your possibilities.

OBEY
YOUR
THIRST

DIRT
This rider is performing a backflip over a large double jump—just one style of dirt riding.

Sprite Sprite
VERTICAL

RAMP RIDING
As this rider shows, you can ramp ride with both wheels firmly on the surface.

First Steps

Practice street riding at the park or anywhere away from traffic. It's important to be confident handling the bike before you move on to harder moves. Learn to jump and bunny hop first. Then you can progress on to flatland, with moves like the decade. Eventually, you may be ready to try dirt or ramp riding.

ROCKET JUMP

The near-vertical rocket jump is easily learned, once you can bunny hop.

GUIDE #3

THE DECADE

1. Roll forward slowly. Pull on both brakes. Rock back onto the back wheel and pull up the front end. **2.** Kick off the seatpost. **3.** Jump around the headtube (the top of the bike), keeping your arms locked. **4.** Land with your other foot on the seatpost. **5.** Put your foot onto the pedal. **6.** – **7.** Release your brakes and ride out.

1.
2.
3.
4.
5.
6.
7.

After you have learned a few basic tricks, it's time to find somewhere to show off your new skills. The best places are public skateparks or tracks with a few jumps.

Your Style

Once you find a small ramp or a jump, spend time figuring out which way you turn and which foot you lead with. This should feel natural, like being left- or right-handed.

FALAFALS
ORANGE JUICE
TROUBLE

Social Life

Bigger parks are supervised and have a variety of ramps. The best ones are indoors, so you can ride them year-round. You can pick up new moves and meet other riders. You may hear about trails and street-riding areas.

KEEP WATCHING

By watching others, you can learn complicated rolling tricks, like this hitchhiker.

GUIDE #4 TRICKS TO TAKE YOU FURTHER

360 Jump

Learn this trick on the ground first. Twist your body, and the bike will follow. The speed you need to twist depends on the distance you jump. Start off with small jumps, then move on to larger ones. Midway through a 360 jump, check to see where you will land. The rotation should end as you bring it in for the landing.

Busdriver

During this trick, you jump and spin the handlebars. Practice barspins on the ground first (roll slowly, lean back a little, and spin). When you're comfortable, try it in the air. Jump, pinch the seat with your knees, spin the bars, catch the bars, land. Be sure to start the busdriver when you're fully in the air. Spinning the bars too early badly affects your jump. This trick isn't easy at first. Always wear a helmet and expect to fall off.

Grinds and Stalls

Stick pegs on your bike and try a few grinds (scraping a part of the bike on an obstacle) along the edges of ramps or along concrete ledges. Then do some stalls (briefly stopping the bike). If you stall on your front peg, that's a toothpick. The nosepick is a front wheel stall. The icepick (shown left) is a stall on the back peg.

The milestone tricks on these pages pushed riding to another level. You may be surprised to learn just how old some of these moves are.

900 AIR
An unbelievable amount of rotation is needed to spin 900 degrees. This is Simon Tabron in midrotation.

PIPE
PIPE
PIPE
PIPE

The Flair

A flair is a backflip with a 180-degree turn added, allowing the rider to reenter forward. Back in 1990, Mat Hoffman performed a backflip fakie on a half-pipe. That means he went straight up the ramp, flipped in the air, and landed backward. The freestyle world was amazed. Three months later, he did a flair 7 feet (2 meters) out of the ramp on only his second attempt.

GOT IT DOWN
Dave Mirra helped perfect the flair's technique.

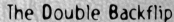

The Double Backflip

This contest winner takes a lot of airtime to fit in the rotations. Jay Miron, nicknamed the Canadian Beast, tried after others failed. After a couple of trips to the emergency room, Jay pulled off the trick on live TV in 1996.

The 900-Degree Aerial

When you're riding a vert ramp (a ramp with completely vertical sides), the idea of fitting in 2½ rotations while in the air may seem far-fetched. In 1989 Mat Hoffman did one in competition. It was only his second attempt, and he had a broken thumb! The 900 is still a fairly rare sight. Hoffman and Simon Tabron are the main riders to pull it off regularly.

CENTRE-PARTING
If this sequence doesn't make any sense it's because a three-sixty backflip doesn't make any sense.
From here on in let this this be known as a Zak Flip.

THE $20,000 FLIP
Steven Murray unleashed the first double flip at the 2001 X Games. He took the first place prize of $20,000.

360 BACKFLIP
Zach Shaw added a 360-degree turn to a backflip jump. The "Zachflip" was born. Other riders are still struggling to do one.

At any skatepark, you will see a variety of ramps. There are full-blown 13-foot (4-meter) half-pipes, miniramps, and simple wedge ramps. The riding on these ramps is as varied as the design of the ramps themselves.

Vert

Vert riding uses the vertical face of a quarter-pipe or half-pipe. It is the oldest and most spectacular form of ramp riding. The true experts of the half-pipe have developed their skills with years of practice. Injuries often happen, especially when new tricks are invented. All the top ramp riders bear the scars to prove it!

WORKING UP
Work on being able to land safely. Then try simple airborne tricks, such as this cancan.

D. Mirra

READY TO LAND
Dave Mirra picks his landing spot carefully after a large air.

GUIDE #5

MINIRAMP RIDING

If you don't want to run the risk of performing tricks on a vert ramp, miniramps are the solution. Many riders use miniramps to practice grinds. Grinding tricks can be performed on the metal coping, or piping, at the edge of the ramp. The platform and walls behind the curved transition are also good for grinding.

SALOMON

MINIRAMPS

A miniramp stops before its slope becomes vertical. This rider is returning backward, or "fakie," from a wall behind the miniramp.

DOUBLE PEG STALL

Miniramps are a popular feature in BMX competitions. This rider has gone up the miniramp, twisted the bike around, and stalled with both pegs on the coping.

Think back to when you first learned to ride a bike. Up and down the pavement. Off the curb. A skid on the gravel. Without realizing it, you were street riding! Do this on a BMX, and you're there.

On the Street

Street riders start by bunny hopping onto and over objects. Next there's manual rolls (wheelies without pedaling), grinds, and stalls. You can use the environment around you to invent new moves. But it's important to respect other people's safety and property.

STREET COURSE

Street contests test riders' skills and imagination. Here, the rider twists the handlebars downward as he exits a ride up a wall (a wall ride).

CONCRETE
At a concrete skatepark, Ian Morris performs a tabletop jump, where he lays the bike flat in the air.

Get Off the Street!

To reduce the damage and risk caused by street riders and skaters, many local skateparks have been built. They have large boxes to jump and flat ledges and sloping rails to grind. As well as being away from the public, they are usually well supervised and maintained.

GUIDE #6

REAL STREET vs. PARK STREET

Extreme sports channels on TV often show so-called BMX street contests. But these contests are staged at special parks rather than on the street. Street riders often dismiss these contests. They feel that tricks on a real street are every bit as good as the spectacular stunts performed by ramp riders.

Real Street?
It would be impossible to perform a trick like this inverted air, just by using the obstacles on a real street.

Real Street!
For a purist street rider, the reward comes from mastering the terrain rather than beating the opposition.

If there's one thing every rider wants to do when first getting on a bike, it's to get off the ground. What better way to do that than by aiming your bike at a sculpted pile of dirt?

Racing or Jumping?

BMX racing is still at the heart of dirt riding and jumping. Riders race against seven other riders on a special track. They try to make it through qualifying races into the finals. In jumping, the aim is simple: go as high as possible, perform a trick, and land smoothly. Many people choose to jump because it involves less pressure than racing. The emphasis is on personal style rather than on winning.

A SPORT FOR ALL

Beginner or expert, male or female, young or old, there will be a race category for you. Put on a helmet and sign up!

GUIDE #7

A BMX TRACK

The ideal BMX track allows for speed, passing, and big jumps. It should be suitable for riders of all abilities but not too easy.

3. Banked turn
1. Starting hill
2. Speed jump

The Trails Scene

Trails riders spend as much time digging as they do riding. They create huge trails full of obstacles. These are built for jumping over and not for racing through. Trails riders prefer to master their skills solo rather than perform for a crowd and a panel of judges.

4. Doubles

STAY RELAXED

A calm approach to jumping is needed. Fight with your bike in the air and it will look bad. The landing will be worse! Aim to land smoothly, ready to tackle the next jump.

GUIDE #8

TRICKS OR STYLE?

Is it better to pull off a simple but stylish jump and land smoothly or try something fancy and land like a ton of bricks? In many dirt jumping contests, this debate can be endless. Ideally, everyone would like to do it all. It's the mark of a great rider!

The Truckdriver
This fast and stylish jump spins 360 degrees while turning the handlebars a full rotation.

Land It!
The tailwhip involves spinning the frame in midair and landing smoothly on the pedals.

Flatland is an often overlooked part of BMX freestyle. TV programs prefer to showcase the more spectacular areas of freestyle. Flatland may not look it, but it's very, very difficult!

FLAT AND DRY
Rider Lincoln Blacksley jumps to switch his feet around, midtrick, while spinning on his front wheel.

Dedicated Riders

Flatland riders have become a closely bonded community. Originality and style are at the core of flatland. Riders must develop their own tricks and combinations. In a contest, riders are generally scored on overall impression. It is often difficult to choose a clear winner. Many flatlanders have chosen to turn their backs on the contest scene. They may ride simply for their own enjoyment.

TSF
HARO

HUMBLE BEGINNINGS
The headstand was an early balancing trick. Flatlanders have moved on to even more complicated moves!

GUIDE #9

BRAKES OR NO BRAKES?
The setup of a flatlander's bike is as individual as his or her style. Some riders remove their brakes. They rely on balance and bike control. Without brakes, moves are harder and less controlled.

Brakes
Stephen Green uses his front brake to change his direction and his position in a front-wheel scuffing trick.

No brakes
With no brakes, Alex Vickers uses his momentum to spin around backward and in circles.

Masters of their Sport

These riders have taken BMX to new extremes. Bravery, imagination, dedication, and years of practice have taken them to the very top of their sport.

THE CHAMP
Mat Hoffman with the winner's trophy at an indoor event in Paris, France.

Mat Hoffman

Perhaps the most daring and innovative half-pipe rider of all time, Mat has invented countless moves. He has devoted himself completely to riding, running contest series, and the Hoffman Bike company. His numerous injuries prove his commitment to the sport.

"THE CONDOR"
Mat Hoffman is an amazingly daring and inventive rider. Here, he performs an inverted air with both hands off the handlebars.

Dave Mirra

Hailing from North Carolina, Dave has won more big vert and street contests than any other rider. He has ten X Games gold medals. He is capable of riding well in virtually every area of BMX.

THE MIRACLE BOY
Dave Mirra demonstrates a busdriver on a half-pipe.

Martti Kuoppa

From Helsinki, Finland, Martti first appeared on the worldwide scene at the World Championships in 1997. He impressed the judges with his own distinctive style. Martti has won countless contests, riding with superhuman speed. His fluid style links impossible-looking tricks in one smooth motion.

SUPERHUMAN
Martti quickly links backward rolling moves like this with other hard tricks.

Jamie Bestwick

Jamie has been a top vert rider since the early 1990s. From Derby, England, he settled in the United States to ride full-time. Jamie endlessly pulls tricks like 540s and flairs both ways, while keeping unbelievable height.

PROVIDENCE.R.I.
GRAVITY
GAMES

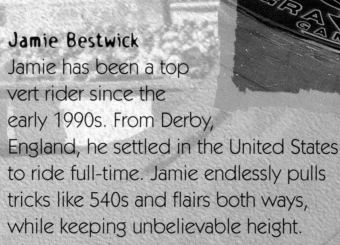

LONG WAY DOWN
Jamie Bestwick spins 540 degrees on his way to first place in the Gravity Games.

Further Reading & Websites

FURTHER READING

Blomquist, Christopher. *BMX in the X Games.* New York: PowerKids Press, 2003.

Deady, Kathleen W. *BMX Bikes.* Mankato, MN: Capstone Press, 2002.

Dick, Scott. *BMX.* Chicago: Heinemann Library, 2002.

Hayhurst, Chris. *Bicycle Stunt Riding!* New York: PowerKids Press, 1999.

Herran, Joe and Ron Thomas. *BMX Riding.* Broomall, PA: Chelsea House Publishers, 2002.

Maurer, Tracy Nelson. *BMX Freestyle.* Vero Beach, FL: Rourke Publishing, 2002.

Nelson, Julie. *BMX Racing and Freestyle.* Austin, TX: Raintree Steck-Vaughn Publishers, 2002.

WEBSITES

BMX Plus! Online
<http://www.bmxplusmag.com>

BMX Trix
<http://www.bmxtrix.com/>

Dig BMX Magazine
<http://www.digbmx.com/>

The Flatlander
<http://www.theflatlander.com/>

Women of Freestyle
<http://www.wofbmx.com/home.html>

Glossary

aerial: a trick on a ramp, where the rider turns in midair to land back on the ramp

fakie: a trick done backward

flip: to spin around in the air backward or forward

forks: the tubes at the front of the bike that connect to the frame and hold the wheel

frame: the main part of the bike, on to which the wheels and seat fit

grind: any trick where a part of the bike, such as the pegs or chain, scrapes (grinds) an obstacle. They can be performed on ramps, ledges, benches, and rails.

gusset: a tube or plate welded onto any part of a frame to add strength. Gussets are usually found behind the headtube and bottom bracket.

half-pipe: a ramp with curved sides that resembles a pipe cut in half

handlebar: the curved metal bar with which you steer a bike

height pole: a measuring device that shows how high a BMX rider jumps

inverted: any trick performed upside down

motocross: a type of motorcycle racing done over rough terrain

180: a half-turn that lands backward. If a move is named with a number, like a 180, 360, 540, or 900, the number refers to the degrees of rotation that the bike goes through.

peg: a tube of hard metal that runs through the center of the wheels. The pegs can be used for grinding and stalling. You can balance on the bike by standing on the pegs.

quarter-pipe: a ramp that is half the size of a half-pipe

stall: a trick that involves momentarily stopping before pulling out of the move. Stalls can be performed on the coping of a ramp, a rail, or a ledge.

trails: a complex set of jumps built purely for jumping

transition: the curved bottom part of a ramp

wheelie: a trick where you lift the front wheel off the ground and cycle along on the back wheel

X Games: a massive annual competition held in the United States, featuring all extreme sports

Index